BORNEO ALIVE

Exploring Sarawak's Rainforest

PRINCIPAL PHOTOGRAPHY:
MAX LAWRENCE

TEXT:
DR. PAUL CHAI

Produced by Hans Höfer
Designed by APA Publications

INSIGHT TOPICS

BorneoAlive

Published by Apa Publications (HK) Limited © 1993
Photography © 1993 individual photographers
All Rights Reserved
Concept by Hans Höfer
Design Direction by V. Barl

All enquiries should be directed to the Project Manager, Borneo Alive,
Höfer Media (Pte) Ltd, 38 Joo Koon Road, Singapore 2262.
Tel: 8612755. Fax: 8616438.
Printed in Singapore by Höfer Press (Pte) Ltd.
ISBN: 962-421-184-1

Contents

Sarawak has some of the finest rainforests in the world and is home to innumerable flora and fauna. It would be impossible to show the entire range of beautiful plants and animals that inhabit the forest, but in this book, Max Lawrence has captured the exotic beauty of the rainforest, enabling those who do not have the opportunity to visit or live in the forest to see and appreciate the animals and the beautiful plants. In essence, the photographs show what can be seen in the forest by any traveller without any effort other than to actually stop and look around.

This is the first book of its kind ever produced on the Sarawak forest and Max Lawrence is fortunate to have Dr. Paul Chai, who is a botanist by profession and attached to my Ministry of Environment and Tourism Sarawak, to co-author this book.

The purpose of this book is to increase rainforest awareness and to show that Sarawak has very beautiful forest that will remain for generations. This book is timely in the sense that the State Government of Sarawak is now endeavouring to promote nature tourism in the State. Numerous national parks and nature reserves have been and are being established where tourists and nature lovers will have an opportunity to see nature in its pristine glory.

Datuk Amar James Wong Kim Min
Minister for Environment and Tourism

THAILAND

MALAYSIA

SUMATRA

SARAWAK

KALIMANTAN

Sarawak

62 miles / 100 km

Mangrove Forest
Swamp Forest
Hill Forest
Hill Forest above 2500 feet
Secondary Vegetation
National Park
Proposed National Park

South China Sea

Bandar Seri Begawan

Menggalong

G. Lumaku 1966

Belu

Kuala Belait

Seria

Benutan

SABAH

Miri

Lambir N.P.

Rumah Gadong

BRUNEI

Mt. Harden 2160

Kuala Sibuti

Niah Caves

Niah N.P.

Rumah Entebang

Gunung Mulu N.P.

G. Mulu ▲ 2377

Bareo

Longbirah

Rumah Lagan

Loagan Bunut N.P.

Similajau N.P.

Tanjong Kidurong

Long Pila

Prop. Pulong Tau N.P.

Bongan-longit

Bintulu

S A R A W A K

Rumah Abang

Belaga

Prop. Usun Apau N.P.

Oya

Kejaman

PULAU BRUIT

Paloh

Ajan

Bukit Batu ▲ 2028

Sibu

Keranji

Mukah

Kanowit

Rajang

Longnawan

Muarebemlelakidau

Sarikei

Song

Baleh

M A L A Y S I A

Cape Datu

Prop. Tanjong Datu N.P.

Teluk Datu

Prop. Santubong N.P.

Kampong Pueh

Gunung Gading N.P.

Sematan

Bako N.P.

Kabong

KAPUAS HULU RANGE

Metulang

Brahim

I N D O N E S I A

Kubah N.P.

Kuching

Bau

Simunjan

Betong

Lupar

Batang Ai N.P.

Mt. Liangpran ▲ 2240

Romo

Bandar Sri Aman

Kaong

Penjawan

Mt. Kerihun ▲ 1980

Tebakang

Telagus

L. Sumpa

Putussibau

Padas

In the heart of Southeast Asia, the pulse of life is intricately bound to some of the world's oldest, most luxuriant rainforests. In Sarawak, these forests and their rivers are still an intimate and inseparable part of the people's lives.

Where many Sarawakians grew up, the forest was the nearest playground. Sometimes it was friend and sometimes foe, but it was always fascinating. As children, we thought it would always be there. Today, we know the rainforests of the world are fighting for survival. With the international spotlight focused on the problems caused by deforestation, Sarawak and its rainforest wealth has not escaped global examination.

Sarawak, one of the two eastern states of the Federation of Malaysia, occupies the southwestern portion of the island of Borneo. It first came into contact with the outside world as early as the 7th century, when its people established barter trading with merchants from China, India and other neighbouring countries. These traders only knew of the country as Borneo as Sarawak did not come into prominence till 1841, after James Brooke arrived to establish the rule of the White Rajahs.

The riches of the rainforest lured traders to Borneo in those years, as it still does today. For the original peoples of Sarawak, the forest provided shelter, food, fuel, medicines and raw materials to build and trade with. Even today, much of Sarawak's ethnic population lives in the forests, in thousands of longhouses and villages by streams and rivers.

These natural waterways meander for hundreds of kilometres before draining into the South China Sea. This dense network of waters also carries fine grains of earth down from the highlands. This is deposited in the lower stretches of the rivers to create rich alluvial plains, like the one the state capital of Kuching has sprung from, or at river mouths to form extensive mudflats colonised by mangroves and fishing villages. Around these rivers, lush rainforest originally covered 75 per cent of Sarawak's total land area. Today, as much as 70 per cent of Sarawak is still under natural, and very varied, forest cover. The range of landscape and geological features in Sarawak gives rise to at least ten major types of forest of different structures and species composition.

This marriage of diverse forest types has created homes for more than 8,000 species of plants and more than 20,000 species of animals, including a myriad of those that chatter, sing and screech.

In the face of the world's diminishing rainforests, the protection and survival of this natural treasure has never been more important.

Here in Sarawak, preservation of a full range of forest habitats is a fundamental part of State Government policy. These forests are totally protected in areas designated as national parks and wildlife sanctuaries.

Sarawak has nine national parks and three wildlife sanctuaries with a total area of 288,719 hectares. In addition, at least eight more national parks and three wildlife sanctuaries are being considered. These, including several extensions to existing parks and sanctuaries, would have an area of 688,619 hectares. When fully established, these protected areas would represent about 7.6 per cent of the existing natural forest estate.

The national parks showcase some of Sarawak's best forests and landscapes. They are accessible to anyone who wishes to explore the wealth and diversity of flora and fauna, or to appreciate the beauty and grandeur of the rainforest.

Photography began for me as a hobby when I was ten years old. My first pictures were published when I was sixteen in what was then New Zealand's premier picture magazine. Around this time I began to think how nice it would be to make it into the pages of *National Geographic* and thus set a standard for my work. I never actively pursued photography as a career but continued to travel around taking pictures that would possibly constitute stock photography. By my mid-twenties, however, I felt there must be more to this photography than stock shots. So I began to look more closely at other photographers' work whose style appealed to me and then going on to meet them.

In the 1970s, I came across the work of Hans Höfer, a recent arrival on the Southeast Asia scene. I showed him material from a trip to Nepal and the next day he offered me my first significant assignment – to photograph Hong Kong for a travel book in his successful *Insight Guides* series. Photography became more purposeful from then on. I began choosing subjects that were more topical and became more involved with images that told stories. I finally began to find a niche in photojournalism. (By the way, I eventually made it into *National Geographic*.)

I come from New Zealand. It's a place where wilderness beckons, where the crisp, familiar scent of nature lifts my soul. I ventured into the Southeast Asian tropical rainforest in the 1970s and found it an utterly mesmerizing experience. Nature soothes my senses, making me feel totally at peace with myself. So, eighteen months ago, when Hans explained to me his concept of a new series of photo books, I thought the Borneo rainforest would be an obvious subject.

Gaps in the canopy light up the forest floor; other parts are shady and cool.

Without any preparation I left for Borneo. An important early contact was Dr Paul Chai, of the Sarawak Ministry of Environment and Tourism. During our first meeting, he mentioned that his Ministry was coincidentally also preparing a book on the same subject and asked if I would be interested in contributing. The Minister, Datuk Amar James Wong, wanted to show that Sarawak is managing its rainforest correctly and not destroying it as some critics have charged.

Our original concept had been to show the natural beauty of the rainforest. With the Ministry's encouragement on the project, I could be guaranteed much support, which is often the key to successful photographs. With Paul Chai having spent 20 years in the Forestry Department, he had the necessary experience and knowledge about the rainforest environment. Paul organised the logistics of the project so that we would cover all the various forest types found in Sarawak. With the assistance of the Forestry Department, which incorporates the national parks and also has jurisdiction over logging concessions, there wasn't any part of Sarawak that I couldn't get to.

My first excursion into the rainforest was a trip to Bako National Park,

Airborne Proboscis monkey.

a relatively small park but interesting in that different forest types can be found there. For several days, I enjoyed wandering about by myself. When first venturing into the forest, one's vision tends to focus on the forest proper. You take in the more general aspects of the surrounding environment – the incessant noise of insects, the fresh smell of the encompassing vegetation, the endless greenery. I often draw an analogy between this and scuba diving. It is almost like being in a different world. Maybe a different dimension. Step into it and the sudden rush of sensation fills your whole being. You want to be part of it, knowing you can never have enough.

On my next trip, I was accompanied by a guide to help me find subject matter. When you give the guide an idea of what you are looking for, it is surprising what he will find. A classic example was on the trail up to a lookout point. Returning, he spotted a beautiful snake that was balanced on a twig, about 30 cm off the ground. We had walked by on the way up without noticing it and I would have walked right by it on the way down had he not pointed it out. With a table-type tripod I was able to lie on the ground and shoot this little fellow from about 20 cm away. It was raining and the guide held a raincoat over me and the camera. The way the snake was balanced was so intriguing. Every now and then, the raindrops would hit the snake, causing it to 'wobble' on its twig. Exposures of half a second are quite safe with a stationary snake. They can remain so still. Another snake photographed that day was the very poisonous Popes Viper. The guide managed to get this snake out of its tree by having it climb onto a long stick and then positioning it so that it could be photographed.

Feeding time for these youngsters.

On another trip through the forest I saw the same species of snake on a walkway. I was by myself this time and followed the procedure of getting a long stick to pick it up and moveing it to a more congenial position. The snake stayed in the same spot for two days and became quite an attraction for all the visitors that happened along the walkway.

The python is an interesting snake, possessing strength that I never thought possible. When it wraps itself around a pig for example, the power it exerts will crush the pig's bones, enabling the snake to swallow it whole. After a meal like that it will lay in a creek or some other place of solitude for up to a month while it slowly digests its quarry. (A python the diameter of a broomstick has enough coiling power to shut off the circulation in your arm!)

It wasn't until I went into the forest with Paul that I discovered what it really was, to look. The forest took on a whole new meaning as the focus of my attention was brought to within a 2- to 3-meter radius of me. I was seeing nature like I had never seen it before and the picture possibilities increased so much that the project now looked destined to succeed.

In the beginning Paul and I had differences as to what would be subject matter for the book. He often wanted to photograph some specimen that had a certain ecological importance in the forest but had little aesthetic appeal. I, of course, would go overboard on a subject that had very little significance in the forest. We devel-

In the law of the jungle, only the fittest survive.

oped a kind of symbiotic relationship whereby Paul would teach me about the forest, and I would help him with his photography. (The philosophy of keeping the photography as uncomplicated as possible leaves very little to be taught). For the most part only two lenses were used – a 60mm macro and a 15mm super-wide. The tripod was used extensively as I never used a flash. I feel that available light gives a truer retention of what the forest looks like. While I inevitably missed out on certain pictures because of not having a flash, I felt it was a worthwhile sacrifice.

Paul, with his extensive contacts in the Forestry Department, was able to arrange for me to go out on species collection trips. This would involve a group of botanists along with labourers, tree climbers and boatmen heading off into the interior to collect various plant species to be brought back to the arboretum. These trips could last up to two weeks and at times we would almost be left to live off the forest.

On one such trip during the fruiting season, many wild boar were 'migrating' through the forest. Several of our Iban guides were understandably eager to hunt the boars as they are a most valuable source of meat. The stealth with which Iban hunt prevented me from following them. They can move so swiftly and quietly through the forest that if I'd gone along, I would not only have made too much noise but I would have probably been left behind, and gotten lost. Having once been lost in the forest, I can assure you that it is not a pleasant experience.

River transport is the most common means of moving about in Borneo. It was also the most dangerous part of the project. While travelling up and down rivers was a tranquil experience most of the time, every now and then we'd encounter a stretch of surging whitewater that had me anticipating a swim for survival.

Users of this waterway can admire nature in all its glory.

I visited Mulu Park on several occasions as it was a place that kept providing me with photographic opportunities. The biggest of Sarawak's national parks is certainly a spectacular area. Park rules stipulate that all visitors must be accompanied by a guide. I was fortunate enough to be provided with a senior guide who was very experienced at working with photographers. He seemed to know exactly what I was looking for and where to find it.

After some time of training my eye to focus on the immediate surrounding, I became quite proficient at finding subject material myself. Oftentimes, I'd still miss a lot as it was vital to concentrate on where my feet were as I walked along the trails. This was particularly important on trails that weren't frequented so often, such as the Mulu Summit trail, where a twisted ankle would have put an immediate stop to my activities.

I had the good fortune to be at Mulu when a helicopter was available. We managed to fly over a large part of the interior. Flying into Bareo, one of the highest settlements in Borneo, was a special treat. There, the climate and soil conditions allow the growing of vegetables rarely found anywhere else in Borneo. The Klabit, the indigenous people of the area, have an ingenious irrigation system which helps sustain a healthy rice harvest, year after year. Their rice has a unique flavour and is the tastiest I have ever tried.

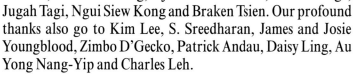

A Penan native making a blowpipe.

The journey to Bareo took us past Batu Lawi, a proposed national park, and then to Usan Apau, another proposed park where three large rivers drop off a plateau to form some of the most spectacular waterfalls I've seen.

While I am not a specialist in nature photography, the pictures in this book came relatively easily. More often than not I would come across a subject, sit with it for a while and just look. A composition would form and then the picture would be taken. I very rarely waited for lighting situations to change as I found from experience that if I moved on, another subject would present itself where the lighting was right.

Sometimes I wasn't so lucky with lighting, as happened with the summit trip to Mulu. Going to the top of Mulu is a gamble if photography is your main aim. The climb from Camp 3 to Camp 4, just below the summit, requires a full day and concentrating on your footing is imperative. For me it rained most of the way up – a blessing in disguise as I didn't have to worry about dehydration. It was bitterly cold towards the top and more than once I asked myself, "What am I doing here?" Photographic opportunities are non-existent when the forest is enveloped in low

Magnificent rainforest canopy in Mulu National Park.

cloud. For the next two days the summit was shrouded in clouds. It's not easy to get the better of nature and I left Camp 4 disappointed at not being able to get a good range of photographs up there. However, we are fortunate to have some of nature specialist Slim Sreedharan's Sarawak pictures in this book and I am deeply grateful to him for this.

Trying to photograph the Rafflesia, the world's largest flower, also requires a certain amount of luck. It flowers for only a few days and has to be fresh to be seen in all its glory. One beautiful specimen we came across had been cut in two by a fallen log, but there is a fine example of the Rafflesia in this book, courtesy of Paul, who also contributed several other photographs.

The object of this book is to show the natural beauty of Sarawak's rainforests in such a way that any visitor can see for himself exactly what I have photographed without too much effort. Just slow down when going through the forest and look about you, in your immediate vicinity. It is comforting to know that this raw, untouched beauty has survived for millenia and will remain for future generations to see. I will certainly return to the rainforest. When I am alone in the forest, it's as if time comes to a standstill.

Paul and I would like to thank all the wonderful Sarawakians who provided so much assistance to make this project a success. Special thanks are due to the Ministry of Environment and Tourism, the Minister Datuk Amar James Wong, Darrell Tsen and Denis Hon; Datuk Leo Chai, Director of the Forestry Department, and his staff: Ting Sie Teck, Mark Yee Shen, Abang Hamid bin Abang Hj. Karim, Chin Fook Hon, Yii Puan Ching, Hj. Othman Ismawi, Rena George,

Jugah Tagi, Ngui Siew Kong and Braken Tsien. Our profound thanks also go to Kim Lee, S. Sreedharan, James and Josie Youngblood, Zimbo D'Gecko, Patrick Andau, Daisy Ling, Au Yong Nang-Yip and Charles Leh.

Max Lawrence

Colour on a cloudy day.

The understorey trees, *Ceriops tagal*, ("tengor") with a dense and extensive network of breathing roots along the river banks.

It isn't easy to convince people how beautiful the mangrove forest is, especially at low tide, when a tangle of roots rise from the soft, slippery mud. With every step you sink ankle- or knee-deep into the slime. While you struggle to pull your feet off the sticky ground, very often without your shoes, you fall victim to swarms of mosquitoes as they constantly attack every inch of your exposed flesh. Yet there is something about this forest that is especially admirable.

Maybe it is sheer amazement that trees actually grow here. The value of the mangrove forest is that it flourishes where no other will. It is a place of scorching sun, flooding tides, sea winds and storms. Yet here is a forest upon which the lives of microbes and men depend on.

Some fishermen come to the mangroves to make a living, others for sports. The mangroves are a nursery for all kinds of fish, crabs, shrimps and prawns. With the fish come the birds – storks, kingfishers, herons and more.

But fishes are not the only reason why men seek the mangroves. The timber of "bakau" (*Rhizophora*) and "berus" (*Bruguiera*) is used locally for piling, charcoal and firewood. Their wood chips are used for the manufacture of textiles, paper and the food flavouring called monosodium glutamate (MSG). A number of plants are important in local medicine. The seeds of "nyireh" (*Xylocarpus*) are used to treat diarrhoea, and the leaves of "pedada" (*Sonneratia caseolaris*), for fever and chicken pox.

If you feel the urge to take a look at these plants, it is possible to walk on the firmer areas of the mangrove mudflats. This activity usually sends tiny fiddler crabs scuttling for their burrows in the mud. Or mudskippers skipping back into the water. Living above them are the crab-eating long-tailed macaque, and the rare leaf-eating proboscis monkey, a protected primate in Sarawak.

Less well-known is the forest's work in claiming land and preventing erosion.

Mangroves develop on newly-formed mudflats in sheltered shores and river mouths. These fresh mudflats can be colonised only by pioneer species of mangrove trees known locally as "perepat" and "pedada" (*Sonneratia alba* and *Sonneratia caseolaris*). After they establish themselves, other mangrove species like the "api-api" (*Avicennia*) and "bakau" (*Rhizophora*) follow. Behind them comes the versatile nipa palm, which thrives on heavy clay soils in the brackish water zone.

How do these plants survive in this unique environment? Through ingenious adaptations. *Sonneratia* and *Avicennia* grow numerous breathing roots called pneumatophores which stick out of the soggy ground to reach air.

The seeds of *Rhizophora* and *Bruguiera* are viviparous. That is, they begin to germinate – to put out a root and shoot – before they fall off the mother tree. The long and pointed root grows so that when the seed falls, it often stabs into the soft mud. This gives it a chance to anchor itself in the ground before the tide can carry it away.

The *Rhizophora* has evolved an interesting way to keep itself steady and upright in the mud – with stilt roots. They arch out and away from the trunk, and into the mud to support the tree against the sweep of changing tides and stormy weather.

Roots like this are designed to disperse the force of the waves. It has been noted by seafarers that the safest place to be during a storm is up a mangrove river. Today, its calm water is a favourite haunt of waterskiing enthusiasts.

27

Mangrove begins life with its pioneer species of *Sonneratia* colonising new mudflats. The roots of *Sonneratia alba* ("perepat") cover the entire mudflat and act as a trap to catch floating seeds of other mangrove trees. The upright breathing roots are important organs for gaseous exchange.

Rhizophora mucronata ("Bakau kurap") thrives on soft river banks behind Sonneratia. Its mature seeds germinate while still attached to the mother tree to produce a shoot and a long pointed root. This root enables the fallen seedling to establish quickly before the tide carries it away.

31

For gaseous exchange, *Bruguiera* produces knee-like breathing roots or pneumatophores.
These roots are 10 to 15 cm above the ground and have many small lenticels on them.

Nipa Palm. Used extensively for roofing material and basket weaving.

Staghorn

The crab-eating long-tailed macaques roam the mudflats in search of food when the tide recedes.

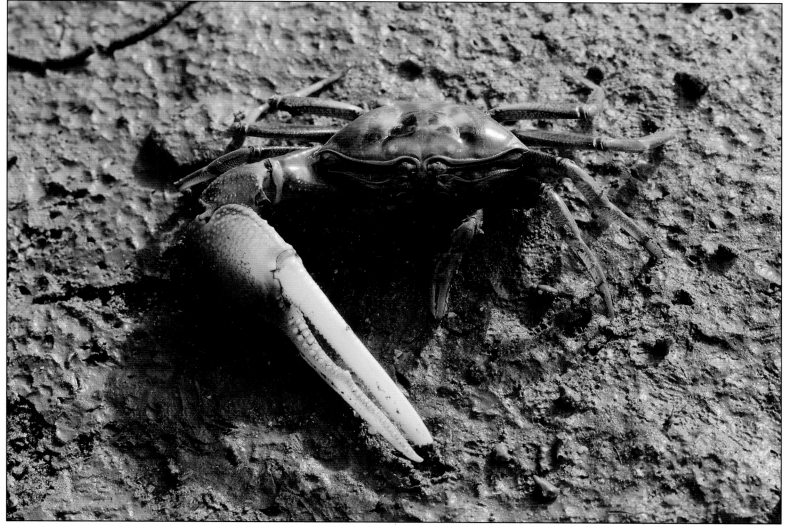

Mud crab (top) and fiddler crab (bottom) are common inhabitants of the mangrove forest.

Brahminy kite.

C*asuarina nobile* ("rhu-ronang") towers over other trees on the cliff top.

When we think of the beach, we hardly ever think of its forest. We go to the beach to play in the sand and surf, or feel the sea breeze on our skin. Beaches are sunlit playgrounds for children and adults alike. Yet as we struggle with our picnic baskets to one, it is not the sunny sand we first look for, but a shady tree to spread our mat under.

Sandy beaches are common along the coast of Sarawak, often accompanied by sandstone cliffs. What plants there are tend to take root behind the beach, just out of reach of the average high tide. Much of the plant life here is concentrated in a narrow belt of trees, shrubs, herbs and creepers of a relatively few simple species.

This narrow band of plants does a lot more than just provide beach goers with convenient shade from the sun. The strip of beach vegetation actually protects the land from being washed away by the sea. Some of the most obvious plants are the tall rows of graceful *Casuarina equisetifolia* trees, the "rhu laut" common at many beaches here. Casuarina trees are protected in Sarawak because they are such guardians of the land. In rough weather, they take such a pounding from the waves that they may be uprooted.

The pounding waves have also eaten into the sandstone cliffs of Bako and Similajau National Parks, and at Tanjong Lobang in Miri. These cliffs are a unique feature of the coastal landscape. At Bako, the constant erosion by tidal waves has cut the rock and revealed beautiful designs formed by iron deposits in the sandstone cliffs.

Only the most stubborn plants take root on the rocks and cliffs here. There is so little to grow in, and so much threatens to tear them away from the tiny nooks of life-giving soil. These small pockets of earth come from semi-decomposed plant matter trapped in rocky cracks and holes. Strong root systems which spread over rocks and reach deep into cracks help to anchor these plants against the wind and water. The amount of soil available often decides how big the plant will grow, or how many there can be.

Whatever grows here has to cope with dry conditions caused by the constant wind and the inability of the sandy ground to hold much water. This has caused many plants to develop thick bark and small thick leathery leaves to prevent excessive loss of water. You will often feel the usually strong and stiff branches and twigs of the small shrubs and undergrowth as you stroll through the forest.

The sandy coastline of Sarawak stretches a total distance of over 500 kilometres, broken in between by rivers, mudflats and mangroves.

❙*pomea pes-caprae* or Morning Glory. A cosmopolitan creeper found on tropical sandy beaches.

 solitary pandan growing out of a vertical cliff face at Bako National Park.

Scaevola sericea – a peculiar flower with petals on the lower side. Juice from the ripe fruit is used by the indigenous people to cure eye disease.

Hibiscus tiliaceus or Sea Hibiscus. One of the more beautiful flowers found on the beach.

49

The cliff vegetation at Bako National Park is a familiar landmark to park visitors. Sandstone cliffs are common along the Sarawak coast.

51

C*ycas rumpii* is a primitive plant that resembles a fern. It is common along some parts of the sandy Sarawak coast.

53

Silver-leaf monkeys are shy animals. Their diet consists of leaves, fruits and flowers. The baby has a different colouration.

The bearded pig roams the beaches at Bako National Park. It is also common in inland forests and is an important source of protein among the inland tribes.

Mixed swamp forest with a dense undergrowth of thorny "pandan".

In coastal and riverine country like Sarawak, peat swamp forest makes up a large percentage of the total forested area – 14 per cent or 1.2 million hectares. Much of this is found in the Rajang and Baram river basins, stretching over 65 kilometers inland. The peat is formed from half-decomposed plant matter in poorly drained areas behind the mangroves.

For all its thorns and dampness, more than 600 species of flowering plants grow here. Precious timber trees are an attraction for man in this forest. Woods like "ramin" (*Gonystylus bancanus*) and "alan" or "meraka" (*Shorea albida*) are favourites and the most common. Men have also come for the milky latex of the "jelutong" tree (*Dyera lowii*) which was used in the dental industry until a better substitute for making dentures was found.
There is actually a particular way these different trees and plants are arranged in a peat swamp forest. Different vegetation types tend to grow in rings around one another.
This pattern of different plants in concentric zones is believed to be due to the decreasing fertility of soils towards the centre of the peat swamp. The outside zones consist of mixed swamp forest and "alan bunga" (*Shorea albida*) forest.

The mixed swamp forest has an uneven canopy with mature trees of different heights. Many species occur here. By contrast the "alan bunga" forest canopy is quite even and simple in structure. It is dominated by the trees which grow to heights of 50 metres or taller. Their grey, cauliflower-like crowns are a very distinctive feature when observed from the air. These two zones produce the bulk of Sarawak's swamp timber.
Trees of *Shorea albida* are most prominent. They have thick straight trunks, big branches supporting a large crown, and thick and extensive buttresses often arch one metre or more above the soggy ground. A trek through the forest often involves clambering or walking (depending on how good you are) over the buttresses. In some places it is difficult to get through the dense undergrowth of the thorny "asam paya" (*Eleiodoxa conferta*) palm without slashing. With these in the way, trekking through the swampy forest is often slow and exhausting.

Yet in spite of all this it is hard to miss the beauty and richness of the forest and its cool and peaceful surroundings. Like the mangroves you marvel at how the seemingly unfavourable and harsh environment is able to support so many types of plant and animal life, all living in complete harmony. Pitcher plants with large handsome pitchers are hard to miss, as are the many species of insects. But there are no leeches to bother you.

Beyond the mixed swamp and "alan bunga" zones, the forest gradually decreases in height and number of species until a stunted open forest of skinny pole-sized trees is reached at the centre of the swamp.
The swamp is rich in animal life. It is the home of many protected species of mammals. Among these are gibbons, tarsiers, flying lemurs, ant eaters and otters. Protected birds include pigeons, herons and hill mynahs or "burong tiong".
It may be difficult to call the peat swamp forest a pleasant one, especially after you have ventured into it. It is the great diversity of plant and animal life that makes it so valuable and special.

The thorny "asam paya" (*Eleiodoxa conferta*) makes walking in the forest very difficult and painful.

60

N*epenthes rafflesiana*, young aerial pitcher.

Nepenthes *rafflesiana*, ground pitcher.

The water plant *Cryptocoryne* is locally common in stagnant pools. It is easily spotted by its attractive flowers which grow out of the water.

Nepenthes ampullaria, aerial pitchers.

Trigonid bees ("engkululut") are important pollinating agents of forest trees. They build their nests in hollow trees which they enter through a narrow entrance made of wax. They are stingless.

Scorpions love to hide in cool, shady places – including jungle boots. Some unfortunate campers have the painful experience of discovering them when they put on their footwear in the morning. They feed on small insects.

Many forest lizards are capable of changing their skin colours to protect themselves against enemies.
This brown Agamid lizard matches the colour of the tree trunk very well.

Stick insects are common but not easy to see. Large ones are up to 20 cm long.

Belian or Borneo ironwood does not require buttresses for support. Cut stumps or trunks left on the ground coppice readily to produce new shoots.

t is hard to escape a ride by longboat on a journey into Sarawak's interior. There is a great temptation to reach out and touch the cool forest waters rushing past the boat. The boat flashes in and out through sunshine and shade. Sometimes it skims over the deep, dark waters. At other times, when the water ripples low over a pebbly bed, it is necessary to get out and help the boatman push it through the shallows. A profusion of plants line the river banks.

In the upper reaches of the rivers, the water is shallow and fast-flowing. Yet some shrubs manage to hold on to and thrive on the banks and the rocky stream beds. These plants have tough stems, branches and roots, and are able to withstand both the swift flow of water and periods of drought. Downstream, big trees lean over the river. Many species have edible fruits which feed the fishes when they ripen and fall into the water. The lower trunks of these trees below the flood level are often thick and rough.

One of these big trees is the common "keruing ensurai" or *Dipterocarpus oblongifolius*. Like the casuarina at the beach forest, this tree is protected because it helps to stop erosion. Its heavy crown also casts plenty of shade and helps to keep the waters cool. Its trunk and higher branches provide homes for many species of epiphytes and climbers.

Sand, silt and clay sediment that escapes the protection of this tree and other plants is washed downriver and eventually settles in the lower stretches of the river as water flow slows down. In the natural order of things, this amount of erosion is quite manageable. It slowly creates flat alluvial plains that are colonised by alluvial forest. Different trees grow here and do so in a pattern of their own.

In the alluvial forest, the lower tree canopy is made of dense, small trees. Much of it is of a uniform height of about 20 to 25 metres. Many trees are heavily laden with climbers of different sizes and species, and epiphytes are common. Palms, ferns and herbs add to the profusion of plants in the undergrowth.

The tallest trees form an uneven emergent canopy at about 40 metres. Big trees like the "kasai" (*Pometia pinnata*) and "benuang" (*Octomeles sumatrana*) reach these heights. Their trunks often grow to one metre in diameter to support the tree.

The forest is also home to the well-known "belian" or Borneo ironwood, *Eusideroxylon zwageri* and *Eusideroxylon malaggangai*. Belian is a very strong and durable timber used locally for heavy construction. It is one main reason why this forest is exploited by man. Another reason is the fertile alluvial soil, ideal for rice cultivation. The flat, open paddy fields in valleys were once covered with such forest before they were cleared for growing rice. Areas abandoned after cultivation take 80 years to return to their original form. This period of regeneration is considered rapid by botanical standards.

Left undisturbed by man, the alluvial forest teems with animal, bird and insect life. Deer and wild boar roam the forest floor, leaving their footprints on the soft ground. Monkeys and hornbills make their home in the top canopy. In between, a great variety of smaller animals and shy jungle birds live. Insects are abundant in number and species and are difficult to miss. But the dreaded leeches are rare here. This forest often floods with the seasonal rains. A heavy downpour could raise the water level by one meter. Leeches are ground-dwelling creatures which love moisture, but not in such quantities.

72

Trees of *Tristania clemenisiae* ("selunsor"), with distinctive brightly coloured bark, are common along the lower stretches of many rivers.

The "aping" palm, *Arenga undulatifolia*, is easily recognised by its long undulating leaves. This palm has a number of uses, such as for thatching and making of blowpipe darts.

Trees of "keruing ensurai" (*Dipterocarpus oblongifolius*) arch over an inland river. Fishes feed on the fallen fruits.

A tree of "kasai" (*Pometia pinnata*) with extensive snake-like buttresses. Its fruits are eaten by birds, mammals, fishes, and also by man.

A colony of *Osmoxylon borneensis* on stream bank with fine sandy alluvium.

Palms are adapted to a wide range of habitats from behind the mangroves
to inland hill forests.

The fern *Dipteris lobbiana* forms large colonies on rocky beds which are periodically flooded with swift-flowing water.

S*alacca* palms are stemless. They produce edible fruits of commerical value.

A species of *Clavaria* with branched fruiting bodies.

Pandanus affinis or "rasau" colonises brackish and fresh water zones upriver from
the mangrove forest, often with its lower parts completely submerged in water.

Less commonly seen is this herb *Tacca borneensis*. It has distinctive and conspicuous purple flowers.

Mushrooms grow on rotten tree trunks and branches. They are an important decomposing agent of the rainforest. Here *Coprinus* sp. grows in small colonies.

Zingiber porphyrosphaera, common along rocky stream banks.

This brown spiny terrapin is easily missed against a background of fallen leaves.

Owls are nocturnal birds and add to the night noise. They perch on low branches waiting for their prey.

Forest insects come in many sizes, colours and shapes. This strange lantern fly, *Pyrops intricata*, is a common inhabitant of Mulu National Park.

90

The defence mechanism of *Eugeissona insignis* ("Pantu"). This palm produces edible sago starch.

For generations, the ethnic people of Sarawak have practised shifting agriculture in the hills. Abandoned rice fields overgrown with secondary jungle are a common feature on hill slopes. There is one forest where rice is never cultivated. This is the kerangas forest or tropical heath forest. "Kerangas" in the Iban language means forest where rice cannot grow. Soil in the kerangas is very sandy and does not hold water which rice needs. Any other available nutrients are quickly washed away or driven deep down to a level where plant roots cannot reach.

This very poor soil supports a community of trees that are small, straight and pole-like. The forest grows to a height of 25 to 30 metres, forming a fairly even canopy. Many small shrubs, saplings and palms grow in the understorey. Missing, though, are many succulent herbs and large climbers because of the dry conditions.

Trees are of hardy species. They have thick bark and small leathery leaves to cut down on water loss. Fallen leaves blanket the forest floor in shades of dry browns, rustling noisily underfoot as you walk over them. The dryness means it takes a long time for them to decompose.

A different type of kerangas forest occurs on the 150-metre high sandstone plateau at Bako National park. The exposed rock surface is uneven. A thin layer of plant litter accumulates in the rocky shallows and pockets of the plateau.

A short scrubby forest takes advantage of this to grow here. The biggest trees are rarely more than 8 metres tall and 15 cm in diameter. Most trees are half this size with very slender stems. In areas of pure sandy soil, there are dense stands of trees which are difficult to walk through because of the large grasses which grow between them.

Again, the thick bark and small leathery leaves are typical of the trees. In this dry, poor environment, other plants find special ways to cope. The common pitcher plants and sundew trap insects for food. Another group of plants get their needs from other plants by becoming parasitic. They grow into host plants and take what they must have to survive from the host. But not all plants that grow on trees and branches are parasitic. Some are epiphytes, merely occupying a niche on a host tree, but not feeding directly from it.

Ant plants are some of the most peculiar epiphytes here. As can be guessed, they have a special relationship with ants. Their roots, leaves and stems have evolved and enlarged to form cavities in which ants live. These thick, fleshy structures also help to store water. In return for a home, the ants protect the plants from possible pests, which includes discouraging overly curious humans from getting too close.

The kerangas forest is pleasant because it is dry, and there are no leeches. Big animals and birds are also scarce. It is also an unlikely place to look for jungle fruits and other produce which are plentiful in the mixed dipterocarp forest. The poor soil, slender trees, lack of game animals and jungle produce have left the forest relatively free from human exploitation and damage.

Kerangas forest at Bako National Park with Mt. Santubong in the distance.

93

95

Inside a Kerangas forest. A *Licuala* fan palm is seen in the foreground.

This handsome fan palm *Licuala orbicularis* is very rare and grows only on sandy clay soil. Its large fan-shaped leaves make good thatching material.

99

Johannesteijsmannia altifrons, a very rare and handsome palm, totally protected in Sarawak and is also listed under CITES (Convention on International Trade in Endangered Species of Wild Flora and Fauna). Its local name "ekor buaya" means crocodile tail, referring to the shape of the leaves.

This ant plant is a slender climber, *Dischidia rafflesiana*. Its normal leaves (above) are small, rounded and succulent. The ants take shelter in the hollows of the modified and enlarged leaves. The ants protect the plant from possible pests.

The kerangas scrub forest at Bako National Park is the home of at least seven species of pitcher plants. The pitchers contain water and digestive enzymes. Fallen insects are quickly drowned and digested.

This pit viper is often seen on low branches close to the ground. Its diet includes frogs and lizards.

The rugged limestone outcrop of Mt. Mulu National Park containing the world's largest cave systems.

Limestone hills and mountains are a natural landmark in parts of Sarawak. Formed under the sea millions of years ago, this limestone has been in existence as hills and mountains for at least five million years. They are usually less than 700 metres in height but Mt. Api in Mt. Mulu National Park peaks at 1,646 metres and is the highest in the region. These rugged hills and mountains have bare cliffs and rock faces. Hardly a suitable place for plants to grow. Yet enough soil collects in cracks, holes and depressions to support a rich variety of plant life. Limestone soils are organic, consisting largely of semi-decomposed plant matter. Many species grow here and nowhere else.

The lower slopes of the limestone hills and mountains are normally strewn with piles of loose rocks. Pockets of deeper soil in between them allow trees as tall as 30 metres to grow. A rich mixture of smaller trees and shrubs form the lower storey, marked at 15 to 20 metres. Trees and plants grow more dense here and the cool forest floor is a favourable place for many types of succulent or fleshy herbs to flourish. These herbs also grow on the rocks. The upper limestone slopes are usually fairly steep and the protruding rocks are sharp. The irregular rock surfaces make it very difficult for soil to accumulate. What soil that does gather supports a forest of medium-sized trees and shrubs. The forest is generally quite open, allowing much light to reach the ground. Shade-loving plants such as orchids and succulent herbs thrive in the cool areas. Many orchids and ferns grow on tree trunks and branches.

Vertical cliffs of a few hundred metres are a common feature of limestone formations. They are fully exposed to the wind and rain and almost devoid of proper soil. Yet these cliff faces are not bare. They are colonised by many small varieties of woody plants. These have strong and efficient root systems which help them to cling on to the rock surfaces and to absorb water and whatever nutrients are available.

Animal life is scarce. Even leeches are rare. Limestone caves, on the other hand, teem with life. These caves are often home to millions of bats and swiftlets, as well as a rich variety of insects which have learned to live in total darkness.
From the swiftlets come nests for the famous birds' nest soup. Guano or bat droppings is good fertilizer and much sought after by pepper farmers. Limestone itself is quarried in Sarawak.

Like the kerangas, limestone forest is safe from exploitation. It is a paradise for botanists and plant lovers to explore and search for rare and interesting plants that are confined only to this forest. Among them are the peculiar one-leaf plant *Monophyllaea*, and many rare orchids and pitcher plants.
Apart from producing birds' nests and guano, limestone caves are fast becoming a tourist attraction in Sarawak. Mulu National Park houses the world's largest cave chambers and passages, while the razor-sharp pinnacles of Mt. Api provide a challenge to anyone who dares to ascend the 1,200-metre mountain slope to the top.

106

The treacherous landscape of this limestone massif is concealed in a dense cover of vegetation.

A sink hole visible only from the air. Its lighted wall and bottom are draped with vegetation.

108

The razor-sharp pinnacles of Mt. Api rising above the summit vegetation at 1,200 metres above sea level.

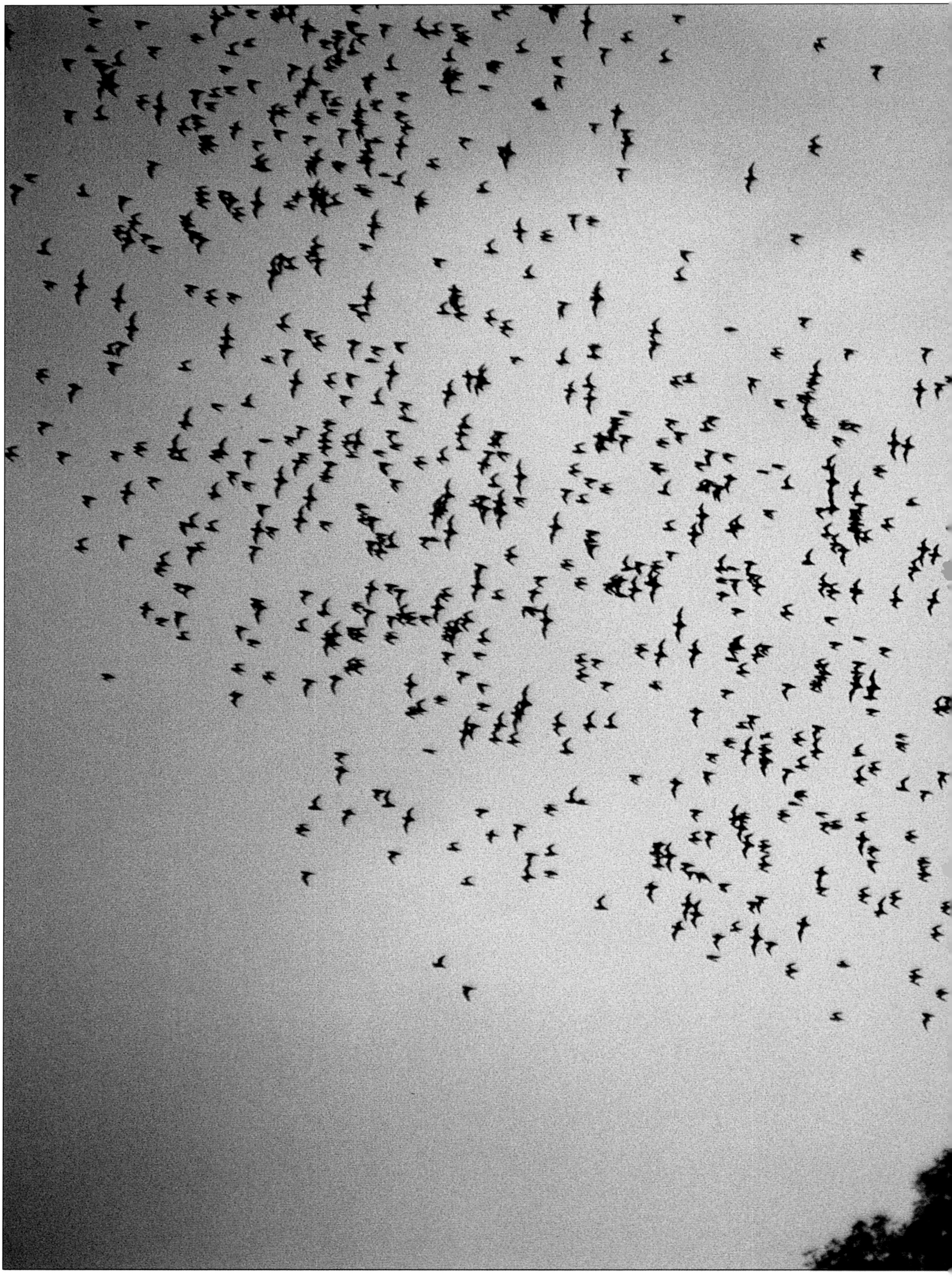

Photo by Slim Sreedharan

Bats leaving Deer Cave. An estimated 500,000 leave in the evening for feeding and return in the morning.

Amorphophallus borneensis, a giant aroid up to 1.5 metres tall. When this plant dies, a large inflorescence appears from the underground tuber.

113

Phalaenopsis violacea, popularly known in Sarawak as Lundu orchid or Orchid Normah, is becoming very rare due to over exploitation by orchid hunters. It was put on the protected plant list in 1991.

Rainbow over a mixed dipterocarp forest.

Beyond the flood plains, the landscape of the interior transforms into rugged rolling hills and mountain ranges. Sarawak's highest mountains are here. Mount Murud rises to 2,430 metres and Mount Mulu to 2,376 metres.

From them, come streams and rivers that carve deep valleys in the mountains. These waterways carry on to meander over the land in a dense, lacy network. Sarawak's largest river, the Batang Rajang, winds 560 kilometres overland before it reaches the sea. The most direct route from its source to the sea, however, is more than a hundred kilometres shorter.

The rising country that rivers like the Batang Rajang is born in is called the interior. Mixed dipterocarp forest dominates here, covering an area of 7.3 million hectares or 84 per cent of total forested area. This forest gets its name from the trees of the family Dipterocarpaceae, which make up about 80 per cent of all wood in this forest. They are hardwood trees that grow tall and straight, branching only towards the top. These features mean many of these trees are greatly sought after by the timber industry – the "meranti" (*Shorea*), "keruing" (*Dipterocarpus*) and "kapur" (*Dryobalanops*).

The variety in the remaining forest is incredible. It is a mix of many tree families. In just one hectare, there are up to 600 trees with a diameter of 10 cm, and as many as 290 species. By contrast, the whole of Britain possesses only 35 species of trees.

The tallest of these rainforest trees form an uneven 'roof' over the forest with their emergent canopy. They grow as high as 60 metres in places. The next tier comes at about 45 metres. This is a more uniform and compact layer, where the bulk of commercial timber trees are found. Medium-sized trees make up the lower storeys between 20 to 30 metres in height.

The forest floor is dark beneath the canopy of all these trees. The shadowed ground is covered by an undergrowth of small trees, saplings, seedlings and a great variety of herbs. Palms, gingers and ferns are common.

Many climbers begin life on the forest floor, searching for a way to grow towards the light-catching canopy. Thorny rattans literally hook and claw their way upwards on growing trees. Epiphytes, plants which grow on other trees, have a different strategy in their search for light. They have minute, powdery seeds that scatter like dust in the wind. With luck, some seeds will land in a hospitable tree. This is how some epiphytes like orchids and ferns colonise the upper branches of big trees where there is more light.

Moving upwards to the steep, narrow ridges and slopes, the forest changes from lowland mixed dipterocarp forest into hill dipterocarp forest. Although the timber trees still dominate, there are fewer species present and they do not grow as big. Small trees, palms and herbs begin to appear. Large climbers start to vanish at the higher elevations, along with birds and animals. The lowland mixed dipterocarp forest is where the fauna is richest, teeming with hundreds of thousands of species of animals, birds and insects. The rare "orang utan" and Bornean gibbon are protected here. So are eight species of hornbills and the beautiful Argus Pheasant, once hunted for its valuable feathers.

It is seldom realised that insects are a very big and important part of the community here. There are thousands of species, many of which are rare, still unknown to science, and whose value to man and our planet are still undiscovered. Through sheer numbers, insects are more often encountered in the forest than large animals and snakes.

The forest may be peaceful but the silence is often broken by the distant calls of the gibbon, the singing and screeching of the birds and the cicadas. When darkness falls, you can enjoy nature's unique symphony of jungle music, performed by numerous insects and frogs. It is an unforgettable experience.

Mixed dipterocarp forest and limestone forest alongside each other in Mulu National Park.

This spectacular waterfall of the Usun Apau Plateau plunges a few hundred meters into the forest below.

119

Bauhinia semibifida is one of the largest lianas of the rainforest. Its thick twisted stem climbs to a height of 40m to reach the forest canopy for light.

Two trees of *Pentace corneri* with large plank buttresses. Buttresses are a characteristic feature of the rainforest.

The twin peaks of Batu Lawi rise above the hill forest in the Kelabit Highland. An area of religious significance to the Kelabit people.

Rice fields at Bareo. Because of its relatively high altitude a rather cool climate prevails, allow-ing cultivation of vegetables and fruits not found elsewhere in the region.

More than 500 species of orchids grow in Sarawak's forests. These flowers of a *Catasetum* are very conspicuous and attractive.

Flower of *Fragraea racemosa* ("tembusu").

Wild gingers are common inhabitants of the shady and wet forest floor. *Achasma* flowers arise
from the underground stems.

Young flowers and fruits of the short-stemmed palm *Pinanga crassipes*.

The spiny rattans are often a nuisance to jungle travellers. The fruits are scaly and many are edible.
Rattans are an economically important produce of the forest. This particular fruit of *Calamus* helps
to alleviate symptoms of malaria.

Close-up of the fruits of *Pinanga crassipes*.

R afflesia.

134

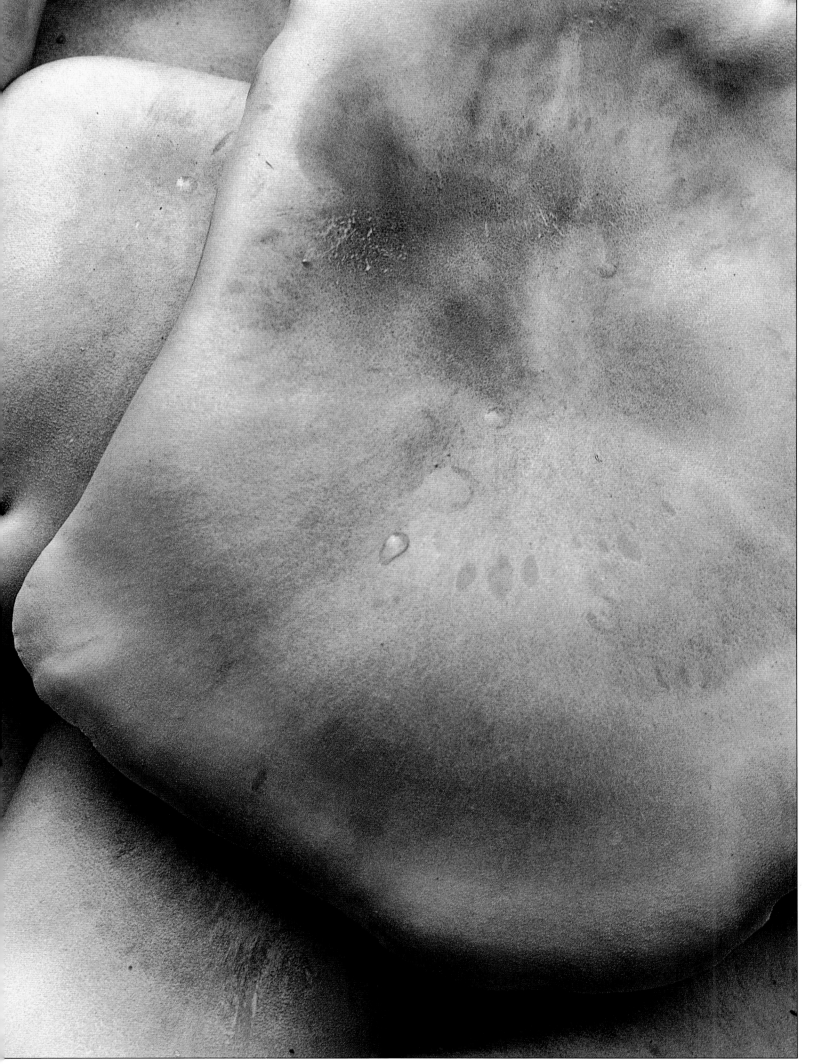

Tricholoma, a large fungus with thick, fleshy fruit bodies.

 A colony of flat millipedes.

The phasmid leaf insect is easily mistaken for a fresh green leaf.

Hawkmoth in camouflage.

139

This twig-like creature is a moth, *Tarsolepis sommeri*.

The binturong – an animal that is easily tamed.

143

The beautiful Argus pheasants were heavily hunted in the past due to the value of their long feathers which the natives used to decorate their headwear. They are now totally protected in Sarawak.

Barking deer ("kijang") are very shy and elusive animals but often fall victim to hunters who attract them by imitating their calls using a leaf whistle.

Orang-utans, man of the forest. Now numbering probably only a few hundred in the remote interior,
this rare mammal is threatened with extinction due to hunting pressure and habitat destruction.

A juvenile orang-utan.

A strange-looking nose-horned frog (*Megophrys* sp.) blends perfectly with the dry leaves.

Forest gecko lays its eggs on the ground.

153

The reticulated python or "ular sawa" (*Python reticulatus*) preys on small and large animals, sometimes including man.

Mosses dripping with water drape tree trunks and branches. They also form a cushion on the ground.

Above the hill forests of high mountains like Murud and Mulu, there exists a forest that is chilly, damp and stunted. It is overgrown with moss that carpets the dark, moist earth and drapes over branches. This is the world between 1,200 metres and 2,000 metres above sea level. It is the montane or mossy forest, home of many species of plants and birds not found in the lowland.

Dense and difficult to penetrate, the band of lower montane forest between 1,200 metres and 1,600 metres is made of trees no more than 40 cm in diameter. The topmost canopy is barely 15 metres high. Below comes a layer of small trees with crooked stems and branches. Beneath this is another layer of plants, a collection of hardy shrubs. Damp mosses grow generously over low stems and hang like webs from taller branches, often dripping with water soaked up from the damp air.

The canopy is even lower in the upper montane forest, barely 10 metres high. Trees here are even more twisted and bent. Weather and soil conditions discourage straight, upward growth. Most trees thrust their branches out to the sides, growing more horizontally than vertically. Woody climbers become rare but small montane shrubs like the Rhododendron and their relatives are everywhere, along with epiphytes like orchids. Sucker shoots sprouting from the ground are also common, adding to the thick growth of plants on the forest. A slender climbing bamboo also grows here.

Aside from birds, animal life in the forest is poor. A survey of Mount Mulu in 1977 recorded 27 species of montane birds. The only mammals present were several species of shrews and mountain rats. In rare encounters with men here, some of these rodents have little fear exploring campsites, occasionally scampering within arm's reach. Charming as these bright-eyed jungle creatures are, they have no hesitation about helping themselves to camp rations that are not secured from their reach.

Visiting the montane forest is a rare treat for those who make it to the top of Sarawak's highest mountains. Up in the cloud-forming zone, the forest is quickly engulfed in thick early morning mist brought in by the cold mountain breeze. Visibility is often only a few metres until the rays of the morning sun filter through the canopy to clear it away.

The high mountain ranges are the birthplace of clouds. At 2,000 metres, the summits are constantly swept by strong winds whipping clouds out of the moist air. At about sunrise or sunset, the change in temperature often conjures clouds out of thin air. The winds may then send them tumbling over the peaks and rolling down the valleys where warmer air and thirsty plants make the grey masses disappear again.

At these altitudes, the days are cool and nights are cold. The harsh and changeable weather means only the toughest and best adapted plants survive. Less than 30 species of shrubs and small plants exist here. The soil is peaty, acidic and weathered, and totally bare of vegetation in some exposed areas.

The biggest trees *Leptospermum flavescens* and *Dacrydium becarii* grow up to 6 metres, contrasting sharply with 60-metre-tall trees of other species in the lowlands. The summit trees are accompanied by a dense, meter-deep layer of shrubs. Among them are herbs like orchids and ferns. The rare montane pitcher plants *Nepenthes lowii*, *Nepenthes muluensis* and *Nepenthes tentaculata* occur here. Unlikely as it may sound, small frogs are known to live in the water-filled pitchers. Animal life is limited to rats, birds and insects.

Camping on the summit is a very chilly experience. Warm clothing and sleeping bags are necessary. The morning remains very windy and cold until mid-day. For some visitors this is the time to enjoy the magnificent views of rolling mountain ranges and forests around.

157

U p in the cloud-forming zone, the mossy forest is cool and wet throughout the day.

A trail through the mossy forest.

 colony of pitcher plants *Nepenthes lowii* growing over the scrub.

N*epenthes tentaculata*, a pitcher plant well suited to the moist organic and acidic soil of the forest.

Rhohodendron quadrasianum

Rhododendron durionifolium

Photo by Slim Sreedharan

Many of the summit plants are dominated by members of the family Ericaceae. *Vaccinium pachydermum* is one of the commoner species.

165